TERRIFIC TANNER

By: Amy Smith

INTRODUCTION:

On September 24, 2001 my world changed forever. It was just a few weeks past 9/11, so everyone was still shaken from the events of that day. I was 6 days late and feeling very frustrated when Tanner finally decided to enter the world. My pregnancy was fairly normal, as was my labor and delivery. But it wasn't long after his birth that we knew something was different about this baby. I'm not sure whether I was in denial or just wanting to believe so badly that he was normal, but I felt myself defending all the obvious signs that pointed to the fact that he wasn't normal. Every Dr.'s appointment was filled with countless questions about why he wasn't developing like he should. To this day, we don't have an answer to that question, so we treat each symptom and problem he's having individually. When he was 5 years old I was sitting in a meeting at his preschool discussing the next step for his education. I sat and listened trying to understand the discussion when one of his workers called him mildly retarded. Instantly I felt a lump in my throat and my eyes began to water. I just kept thinking, my child, retarded. I finished the meeting, hurried to the car as tears started streaming down my face. I just sat there for a while and had a good cry. I had always been so strong when it came to Tanner but for some reason those words were tough. After the tears I decided I needed to focus on the positive things in Tanner's life. Some days are harder than others but overall, our family has adjusted very well to having a special child in our home.

Through genetic testing we have discovered that Tanner is missing 12-15 genes on his 3rd chromosome. A rare finding, with no name to diagnosis his condition. We will probably never know why this happened as my husband and my genetic tests were normal. We've dealt with life threatening seizures, developmental delays, speech delays, surgeries, etc. It's just a part of life for us. We never know what's around the corner. Having a child like Tanner has taught us so many lessons. So every challenge and trial we face we are reminded that every day is a gift.

It's my pleasure to share with you................. "TERRIFIC TANNER".

Dedicated to Minnie Hamilton Bagley:

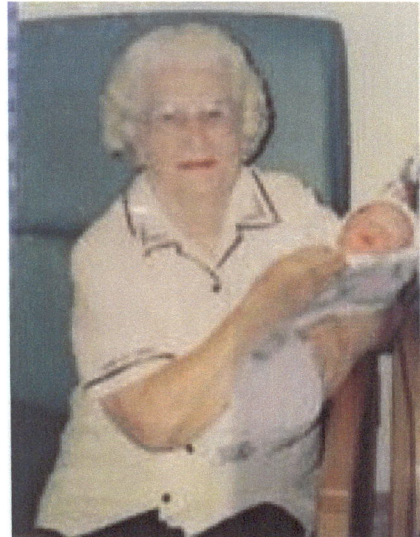

This book is dedicated to one of the most special women in my life......
 Minnie Hamilton Gain Bagley. Her example of patience and unconditional love
has helped me on numerous occasions to endure the many trials of my life.
Before I knew that Tanner was going to be a special needs child, we had decided
that he would be named Tanner Hamilton Smith. Hamilton being my Grandma's
middle name and her mother's maiden name. I don't believe that this was just
 by chance. I believe that we were inspired to help remind us every day that
Tanner is a gift and to treat him as just that. My Grandma babysat Tanner
for us until he started attending his preschool. It was such a blessing to have
 her care for him while we worked. She gave him so much love and attention
that when we went to pick him up after work he wanted to stay with her.
 She was so patient, gentle and kind with him. It helps me be a better mom
because of her example. Whenever I feel myself get stressed or impatient,
I often think of her and it helps me to take a deep breath and get myself
 together again. I will forever be grateful for being blessed with such an
amazing Grandmother!!

What makes Tanner "Terrific" you ask? Oh there are so many things, but mostly because he is one of a kind. Yep, that's right he has been extra special since the day he was born. Tanner's had some very unique challenges to overcome but is one of the happiest kids you will ever meet.

Tanner grew just like all babies but when it came to milestones like holding his head up, rolling over, sitting, crawling and walking he was on his own schedule. He had the cutest dark brown eyes and hair with a sweet smile on a larger than average head. He had this skinny long body with low muscle tone. His dad called him a noodle. When he was one year old the pediatrician told his parents it was time to see a specialist.

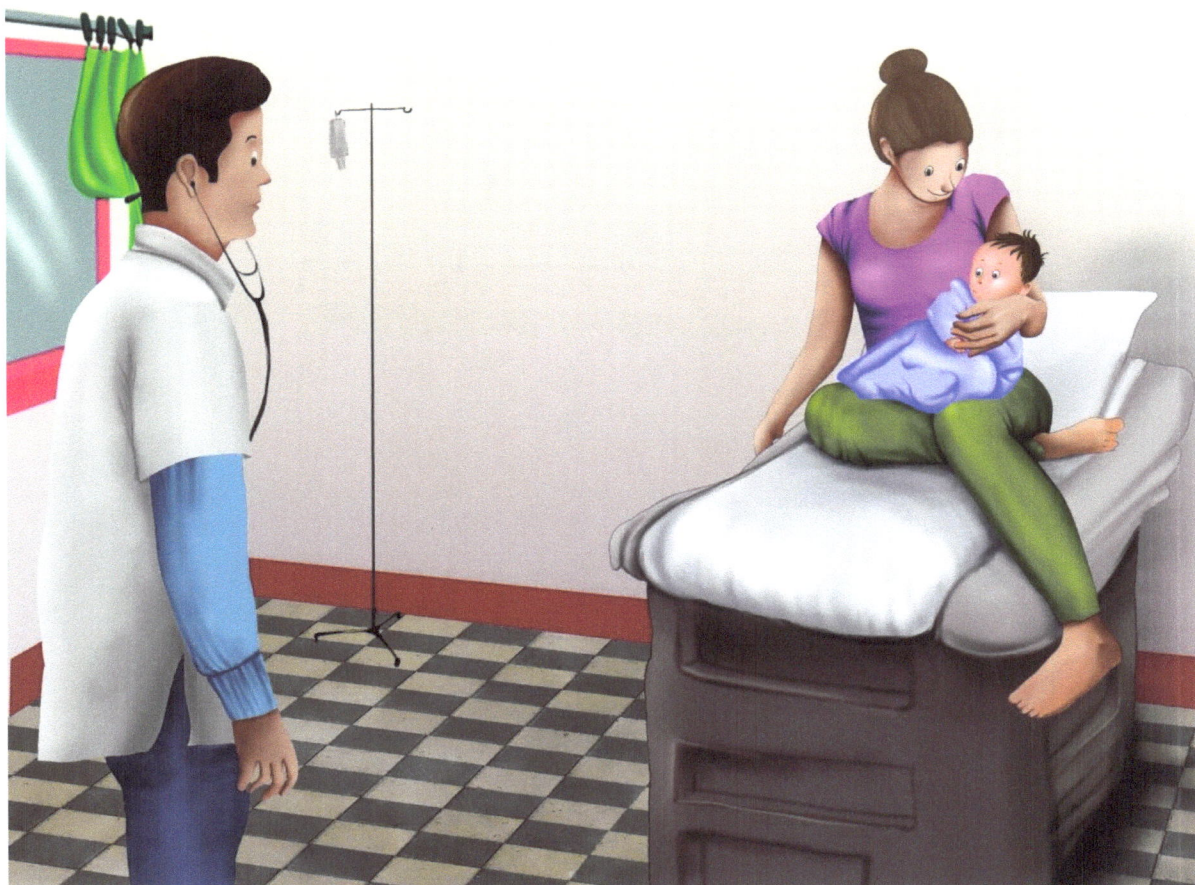

The coolest thing happened at the specialist office. The Dr. walked in and did the silliest thing. He hit himself on the head with a reflex hammer and Tanner started laughing so hard he almost fell off his mom's lap. The Dr. did a few other tests and gave him a thorough exam. It was a good visit, but they weren't able to figure out why he was different. The Dr. referred him to some special people to help him progress and would follow up later.

Tanner worked with his special helpers and continued to grow and progress but he was still delayed in his development. Every day he would wait outside with his mom for his helpers to show up. He drove his battery operated tractor all over the yard. His helpers were amazed that he could hardly keep his balance to walk but when he was on his toy tractor, he could drive it everywhere. He maneuvered around obstacles and backed up like he had been driving for years.

When he was 3 he began attending a pre-school with other kids that had special needs like him. It wasn't easy at first but pretty soon he adjusted and found it to be a fun place to play. In fact, getting on the bus and riding to and from school was his favorite part of the day. His school had lots of cool playground equipment and the workers were so helpful. His favorite person was the maintenance worker. He absolutely admired him because he was in charge of fire drills. It was the highlight of Tanner's school experience. He told everyone that someday he would come back and be in charge of pulling the alarm.

Before too long it was time for Tanner to attend public school. He was so excited because he had an older brother who went to this school. His brother was good about looking after him and making sure that everyone treated him kind. Tanner was popular right away because all his brother's friends and classmates would wave at him in the cafeteria and on the playground. Kindergarten was an amazing place where he met all kinds of new kids and got to play on the best playground. Tanner was so terrific that he got to complete 2 years of kindergarten.

Tanner loved his play time. When he came home from school he spent all his time in his sand box with every kind of tractor and heavy equipment toy you could think of. He spent hours digging in the sand, pushing dirt around and pretending he was a farmer.

He likes to take branches from the orchard and dig them into the ground pretending that it is his orchard. He takes his play harvester out to the grass and pretends he is cutting his rice. He tells his parents that he is going to be a farmer when he grows up. Tanner loves the outdoors and wants to be outside until the sun goes down.

Fall is a magical time for Tanner for many reasons but his favorite thing about fall is harvest. He looks forward to the day that the shakers come to our orchard and shake our walnut trees. He sits outside and watches them for hours. First, they shake the nuts from the trees, next the sweepers come around and sweep them into a pile and lastly the tractor comes around to pick up all the nuts. He loves to ride out to the hullers and watch the nuts get loaded in the bins. He also loves to watch the harvesters cutting the rice. They start in the morning and work all day long after it's dark. He likes to go for a ride in the harvester and watch the rice get loaded into the bank out truck.

On a rainy day you might catch Tanner lining up all his trucks like they are in a parade. He drives them all over the house telling everyone to watch the parade. Sometimes he even puts candy on the back of a truck so he can throw candy to the pretend people watching. He loves to watch movies also, and memorizes his favorite lines to repeat to everyone later. He will sit for hours sorting beads in containers while he watches his favorite shows. Tanner loves to make craft projects and work with wood. He has his own tool box with his own tools.

In the castle, up high on a hill, far, far away is one of Tanner's favorite characters. Tanner's eyebrows lift and his eye's wander side to side when he hears the organ play. His hands come together and he starts rubbing them back and forth as he watches the bats fly around. He could watch a movie of "The Count" over and over again with the same reaction. He repeats all the lines from the movie and asks everyone to watch "The Count" count. His fascination with this character is priceless.

Tanner loves the water. When he gets in the bath tub he lays on his back putting his head under water with just his mouth, nose and eyes out of water. He likes to stay in the bath for so long that the water turns cold and his toes and fingers look like prunes. When he swims he likes to keep his head under water for as long as possible. He loves how the water blocks out all the noise from around him.

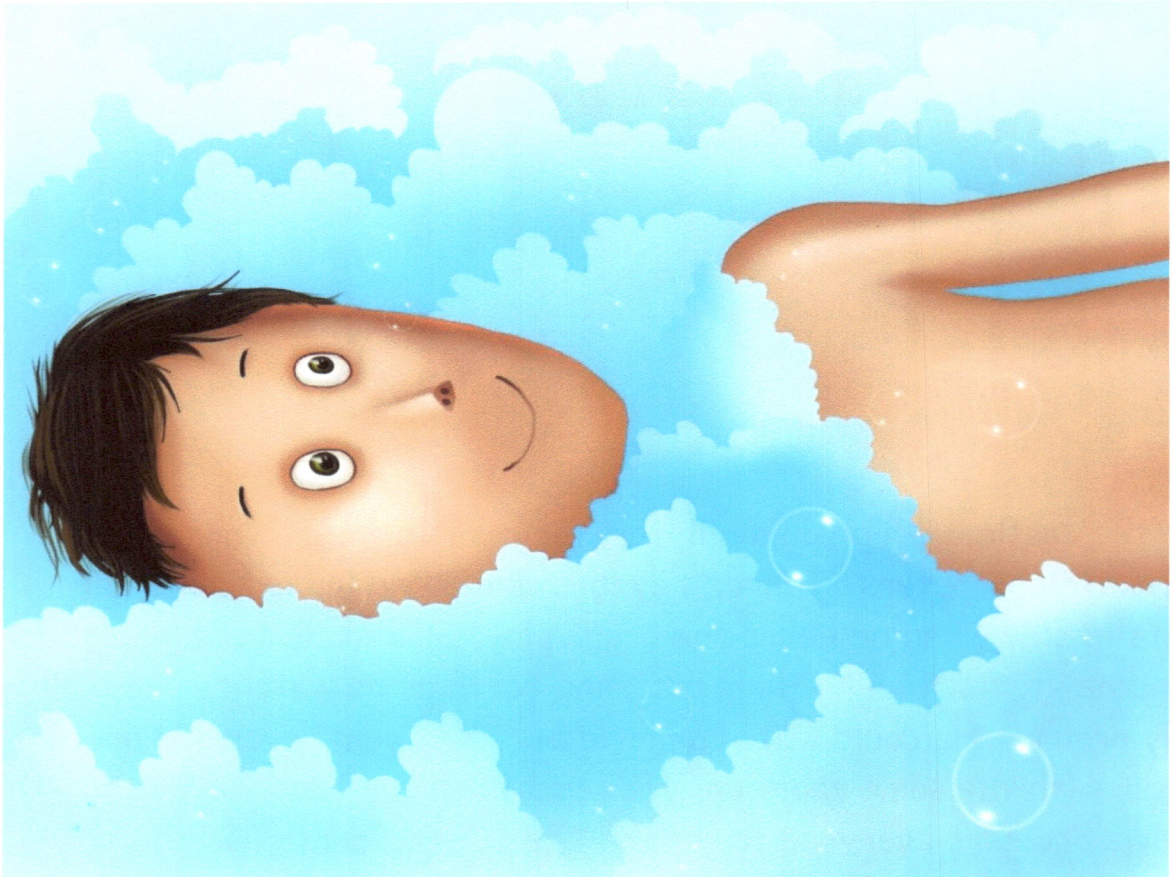

His first year on the swim team, he scared his dad to death.
It was the first meet and he was competing in the back stroke.
Tanner didn't care about proper technique he just swam because
he liked the water. His back stroke was an underwater backstroke.
His dad almost jumped in the pool thinking he was drowning. Tanner
looked up from under the water and gave a big smile. Everyone felt
relieved that he wasn't drowning but they had never seen anyone
swim the back stroke quite like that. Every race Tanner would be
the last one but always finished with a big smile.

Tanner was feeling good about being the youngest in his family. He got lots of attention not only because he was terrific but because he was the youngest. One day he noticed it was getting more difficult to sit in his moms lap and she had a bump on her belly. His parents would talk about a baby but he didn't understand that they meant in their family.

At the hospital he got to meet and hold his new baby brother.
Everyone kept telling him to be gentle and careful around the new
 baby. Pretty soon he realized it was pretty cool to have a little
brother and helping mom with him was fun. He was so sweet with
 his baby brother. He loved to smell his head and kiss him gently.

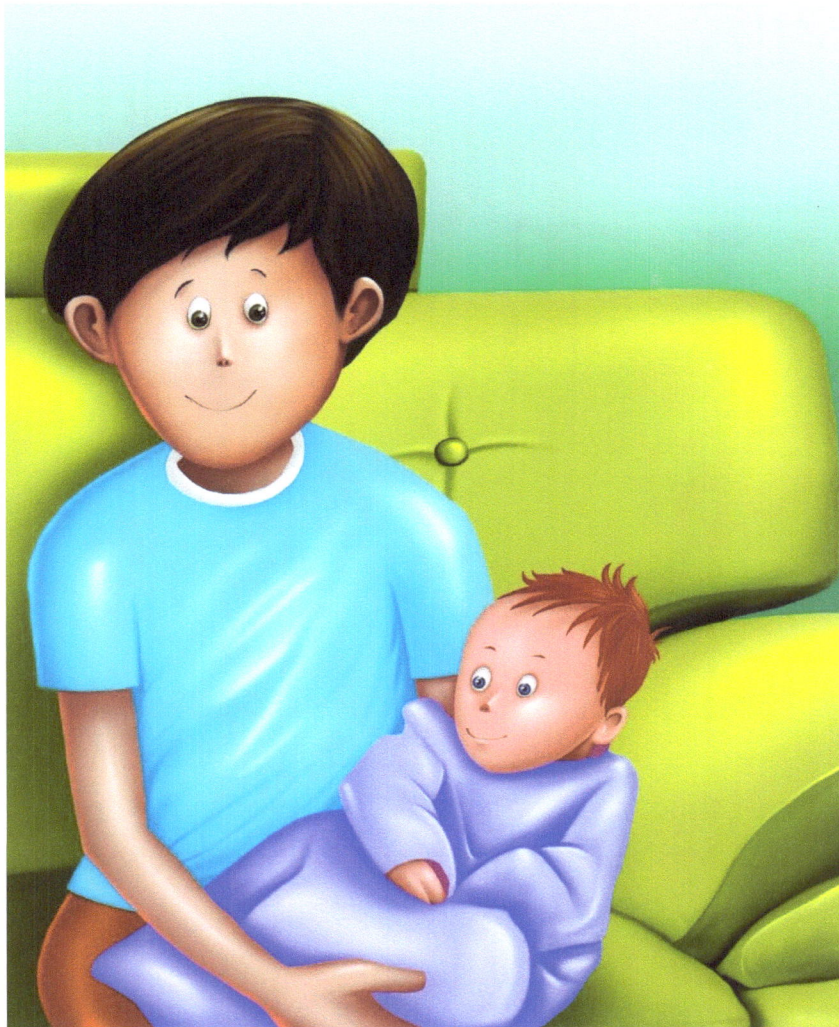

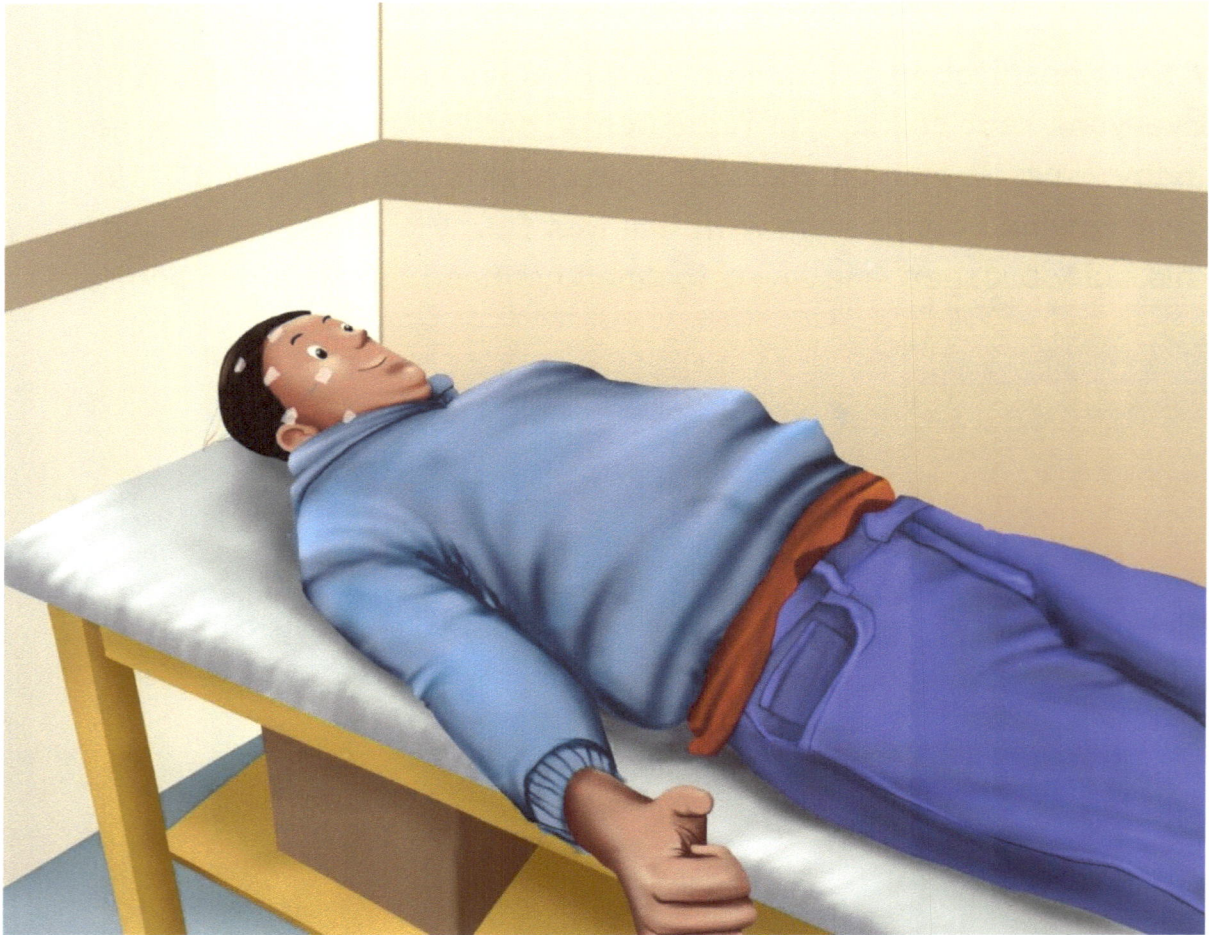

A few times Tanner has had to spend some time in a hospital for children. He even rode in a medical helicopter twice and ambulance 4 times. The visits to the hospital and doctor's office make him very tired. He has many different doctors he has to see, asking all kinds of questions to his parents and having him try really interesting tasks.

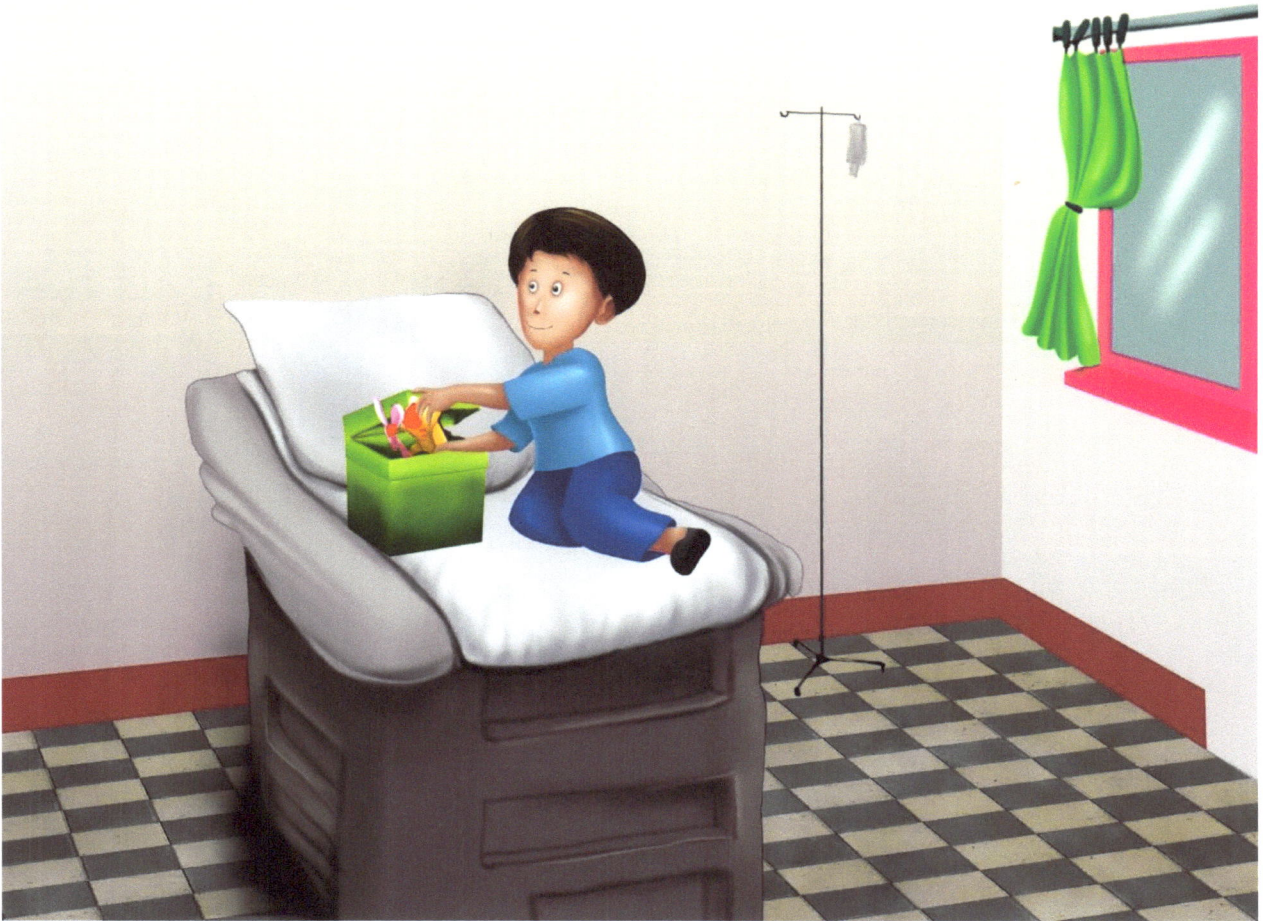

He has had several tests to endure with some being very uncomfortable, making it hard to stay strong. He worries every time he has to go to the doctor and asks the whole time if he has to get poked with a needle. Picking out a sticker or small toy is his favorite part. His nurse or technician had better not forget because he will hang around their office until they remember.

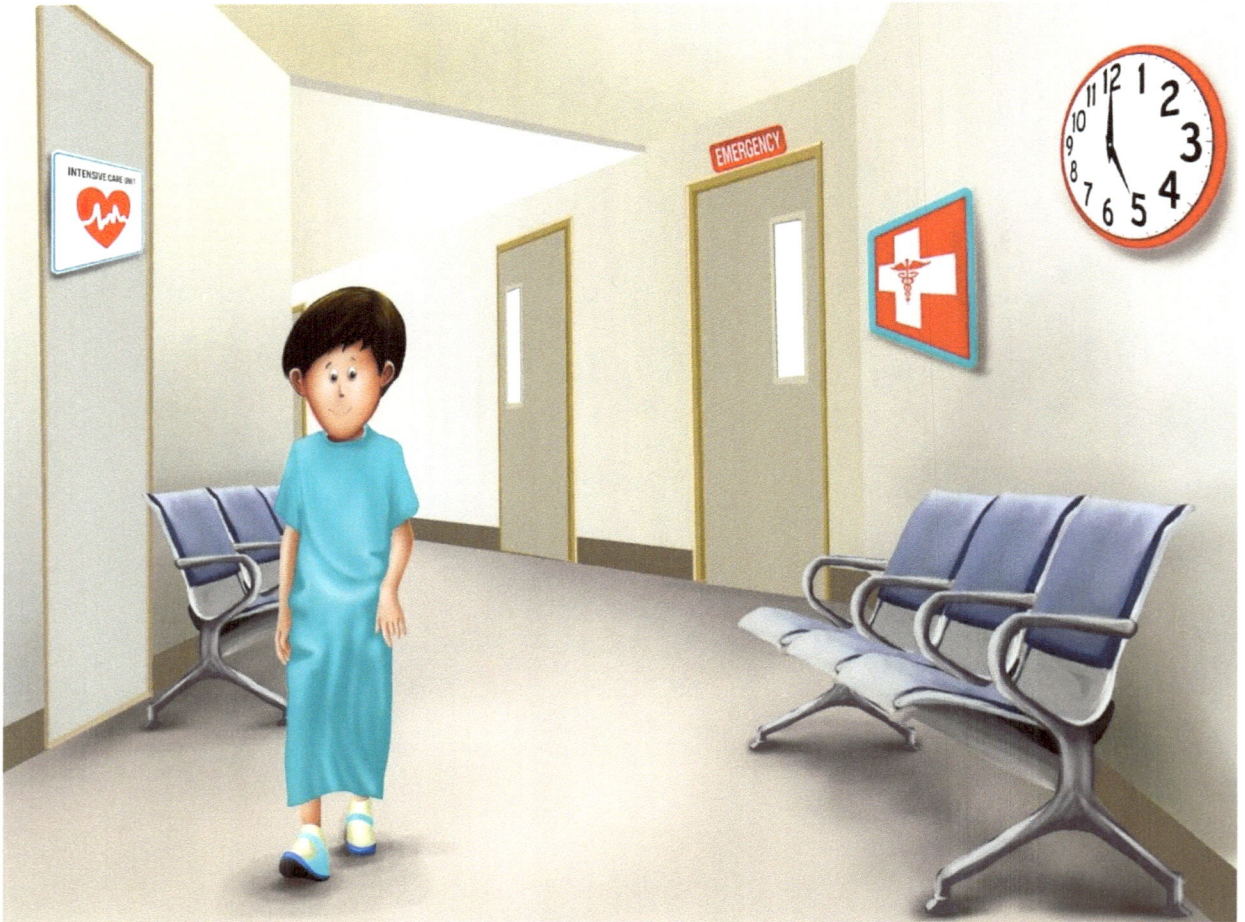

One year Tanner had a seizure two days before Christmas. He was four years old and very excited that Christmas was only a few days away. A tradition on his mom's side of the family was to visit a pizza place with games and rides on Christmas Eve. His mom had taken his brothers and him to spend the night at his Aunt's house so she could do some last minute shopping. While she was out, Tanner had a seizure. They took him to the hospital and the Dr. sent him to the children's hospital where he had been treated several times before. He had to spend the night which meant that he would miss the Christmas Eve festivities. He was feeling sad and decided he would go search the hallway of the hospital for the Dr. When he found him he told him he wanted to go home. The Dr. was so sweet and made the nurses quickly get him discharged. The nurses giggled as they read his parents the discharge summary. They asked if Tanner could come back and get the Dr's to work that fast every day.

Tanner looks forward to Christmas every year and pretends he is Santa Claus. In fact, one year he was Santa for Halloween. He loves to talk about working in the toy shop and pretends he is making toys for the good boys and girls. But be careful, if you are not nice, he will quickly put you on the naughty list.

Tanner gets so excited during the month of December. When he comes home from school he checks to see if there are any new presents under the tree. He writes letters to Santa all month and asks his mom to mail the letters to the North Pole. Just when Santa has all his gifts ready for Christmas, Tanner writes another letter and Santa has to rush around to try to fulfill his wishes.

Sometimes it's not fun or easy being Tanner. Some days he would just like to forget about all his struggles, aches and pains. Recently, he was diagnosed with scoliosis, which causes his back to hurt and he also has had to endure several procedures to correct his teeth. But Tanner does the best he can and tries not to have too many melt downs. Just when things seem to be too hard for him, he is able to find something funny to talk about and before long he is smiling again. Tanner is also sensitive to those around him and longs for everyone to be happy. He is known for his sweet notes or gifts to make that special someone feel loved.

Tanner has a funny sense of humor saying some of the craziest things. He remembers the funniest things about people and he often compares real people to movie characters. Sometimes, it makes his parents nervous, but mostly it gives everyone around him a good laugh.

He has the most infectious laugh. Sometimes he will be quietly sitting and next thing you know he is laughing to himself because he thought of something that happened. When he tries to explain why he is laughing, he can't get the words out. He is so entertaining and is fun to hang out with.

Tanner reminds everyone around him that life is precious and to do the best you can with the challenges you face. Not everything about Tanner is terrific but with all the many things he's had to endure, Tanner still finds a way to bring a smile to everyone's face with his funny sense of humor and his sweet personality.
That makes my Tanner TERRIFIC!!!

My hope is that this book will do several things. First, I hope that it will help bring awareness to the challenges and trials those families with special needs children face day to day. It's not easy and no one asked for what they were given. We're all just doing our best under our current circumstances. Second, I hope that families with special needs kids will see that they are not alone. Every situation is different but understand that many families are facing similar challenges. Lastly, I hope that those with special needs children can celebrate that you are blessed to have this child in your home. I truly believe that God places these children in homes for our benefit. The lessons and blessings you receive from these children will far outweigh any challenges you will face. We all have days and times that we feel overwhelmed but in the big picture it's minimal compared to the lessons they teach us. It is my prayer that families will find renewed strength, hope and love as they care for these special children.

The Smith Family

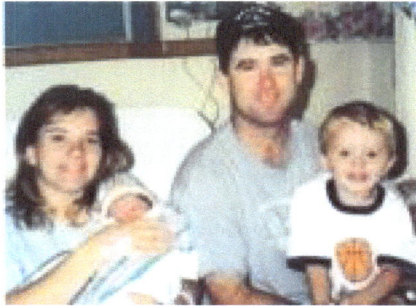

Travis, Amy, Brenden, Tanner and Brady

"TERRIFIC TANNER"

adventure books will be available for your viewing pleasure in the near future!

Terrific Tanner Goes to the County Fair
Terrific Tanner Celebrates Halloween
Terrific Tanner Wants to be a Farmer
Terrific Tanner Celebrates Christmas
Terrific Tanner Plays Baseball

.......................and many more adventures!!!!!

www.ingramcontent.com/pod-product-compliance
Lightning Source LLC
Chambersburg PA
CBHW060815090426
42737CB00002B/75